King Julien and the Rain Dance

Mort

Timo

King Julien

Maurice

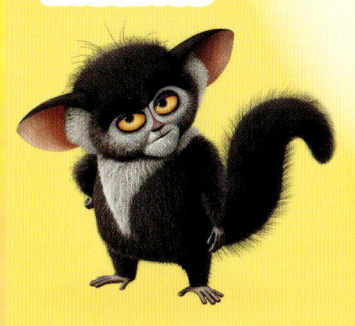

Masikura

Adapted by Cas Lester

It was a scorching hot day, and it hadn't rained for ages.

"We need rain!" said Masikura.

"But don't worry," she said. "Lift up your buckets to the sky, because King Julien will do a rain dance!"

King Julien was stuck. He couldn't remember the steps. "I'll just make something up!" he said.

"No! You have to perform the dance properly, because otherwise it won't rain!" explained Maurice.

"Okay," sighed King Julien. "But I can't dance without Boom Box."

Music blasted from Boom Box as King Julien danced, and dark clouds began to cover the sky.

Suddenly, Boom Box broke! King Julien stopped dancing and rushed over to Boom Box.

"Don't stop the rain dance," begged Masikura.

"Boom Box is dead!" sobbed King Julien. "I will never dance again!"

"I will miss you, Boom Box," sighed King Julien. Then he pushed it down the hill to the rubbish dump!

There was a loud OUCH!

Ouch!

Oops!

"Help!" yelled a voice. It was Timo! King Julien rushed to rescue him.

"Boom Box is broken," King Julien told Timo. "I can mend Boom Box, because I am a *scientist*," said Timo.

Back in his lab, Timo put new batteries into Boom Box.

"It's a miracle!" cried King Julien, as music blared out again!

"No, it's *science*!" laughed Timo.

"Science can do anything!" he said.

"Anything?" asked Julien. "Hmm …"

Meanwhile, all the lemurs were in a terrible panic because it still hadn't rained.

"Calm down!" said King Julien. "Science can do anything!"

King Julien showed the lemurs some machines Timo had made.

Whoosh!

Whir!

The lemurs thought the machines were incredible!

Yum!

"Stop!" said Masikura. "We don't need all those machines. We need *rain*."

King Julien wasn't interested, because Mort was tickling his feet with an electric toothbrush!

Suddenly the toothbrush ran out of power. Timo plugged in the charger, but there were too many plugs everywhere.

The plugs started over-heating.

Fire!

Flames shot along the wires!

"Dig here! We will find water!" cried Masikura. Quickly, the lemurs dug a deep hole, and dropped a hose into the water at the bottom.

Splosh!

Timo made a pump ... but the hose was blocked!

"Don't panic! I can fix this hose pipe with my rain dance!" cried King Julien.

"Slide, glide, shake it to the side!" he sang.

Whoosh!

The water poured down from the pump and put out the fire!

23

Then it started to rain properly!

So they all danced together!